E(EEK)CCLESIASTES

E(EEK)CCLESIASTES

Finding Meaning in a Meaningless Life

Joyce H. Hondru

ELM HILL

A Division of
HarperCollins Christian Publishing

www.elmhillbooks.com

E(eek)cclesiastes
Finding Meaning in a Meaningless Life

Published in Nashville, Tennessee, by Elm Hill, an imprint of Thomas Nelson. Elm Hill and Thomas Nelson are registered trademarks of HarperCollins Christian Publishing, Inc.

Elm Hill titles may be purchased in bulk for educational, business, fund-raising, or sales promotional use. For information, please e-mail SpecialMarkets@ ThomasNelson.com.

Library of Congress Cataloging-in-Publication Data

Library Congress Control Number: 2018951385

ISBN 978-1-595558299 (Paperback)
ISBN 978-1-595558145 (Hardbound)
ISBN 978-1-595558305 (eBook)

CONTENTS

Dedicated to my husband, Bryan Hondru,
because he gets me.

INTRODUCTION

Ecclesiastes is an odd duck. It is, at least in my opinion, one of the strangest books in the Bible.

However, since I believe in God's divine intervention in making sure that all the books in the Bible are there to help us understand Him better, I'm guessing it is included for a good reason.

You may not be at all familiar with Ecclesiastes since it isn't a text from which many sermons are preached (in my experience anyway). Or you may not know much about it because it is in the Old Testament or because no one has ever recommended it to you. However, this is precisely why I chose it. Personally, I wanted to delve into this rather obscure, at times depressing, book to see what gems of wisdom I could find—and I wanted to take you along for the ride.

If you haven't read this book before (you will find it just after Proverbs) please, please don't get discouraged! Even though the author of this book continually makes you think that everything about this life is "meaningless," remember the subtitle of this study: *Finding Meaning in a "Meaningless" Life.*

At times, we all struggle with life's meaning, so walking through this crazy book together should <u>encourage</u> us more than <u>discourage</u> us. In any case, that is my hope and prayer!

Keep in mind, though, as with the other studies I have written, I don't typically consult a lot of theological commentaries or biblical reference books. The reason for this is simple: I want to read the Word of God and hear what the Holy Spirit is saying to me. Therefore, please don't expect an overly scholarly book. I am neither a biblical scholar nor a theologian. Thus, if anything you read herein conflicts with things you have read prior to this book or with sermons you have heard before, don't fret. All scripture is somewhat open to interpretation, and my joy comes from taking it at face value and waiting to see what God reveals to me. Then I trust that He will allow both of us to learn from that revelation.

It is also important to note that this isn't a verse-by-verse study of this book. There are a lot of good commentaries that will help clarify, if you want to more clearly understand, any specific verse that gives you pause, or you simply don't understand. In fact, the footnotes of many Bibles offer help. Mine, though, is an overview of this most interesting, at times perplexing, book, in which I have chosen to focus on what I felt were the most relevant points.

Finally, as with my other studies, I believe it is most beneficial if this study is done within a small group (even though you could do it by yourself). However, the opinions, questions, and insights of others stir thought and discussion that cannot be obtained when doing the study alone. I also feel that if you are doing the study in a small group, it is good to read the paragraphs (what I have written) out loud, along with the questions. This is helpful for two reasons. One, reading the verbiage that goes along with the questions will help maintain the flow of the study and may stimulate deeper discussion. Two, reading this information for a second or third time helps reinforce (as repetition always does) what is being said and should help you better retain the message and/or its key points. No matter how you approach this study, though, may you grow closer to Christ as you study his Word.

A GRUMPY OLD MAN

ECCLESIASTES
CHAPTERS 1 AND 2

Hmmmm, what an interesting couple of chapters, right? Life, it seems, is meaningless. And just to make sure the reader doesn't miss this point, my Bible comes with these headings:

Everything Is Meaningless
Wisdom Is Meaningless
Pleasures Are Meaningless
Wisdom and Folly Are Meaningless
Toil Is Meaningless

Boy, what a great way to start a study! Stick with me, though. I promise it will get better.

But before we begin dissecting these first two chapters, I think it is important to reflect on the person who wrote this book. Unfortunately, though, as is often the case with scripture, theologians disagree on who that person might be. However, for the sake of argument, and since the opening line says, "The words of the Teacher (Preacher), son of David, king of Jerusalem..." and verse 12 states "I, the Teacher (Preacher), was king over Israel..." I suggest we follow the more traditional belief that it was King Solomon (the son of David), who authored this book.

(Keep in mind, it is not overly important that we agree on this book's authorship, but it is important, however, that we agree that all scripture is "God-breathed" and that this book, therefore [whoever wrote it], is included in the Holy Bible with a purpose of helping us learn more about God, and ourselves, as we relate to Him.)

"All Scripture is God-breathed and is useful for teaching, rebuking, correcting and training in righteousness, so that the servant of God may be thoroughly equipped for every good work."
(2 TIMOTHY 3:16–17, NIV)

So, a brief background (or history lesson, if you will) on King Solomon:

1. Many, many years before Solomon was born there was a woman who was barren, who desperately wanted a child. Who was she and what did she promise God if He gave her a son according to **1 Samuel 1:10–11**?

2. What was the outcome of Hannah's prayer according to **1 Samuel 1:20**?

3. Did Hannah keep her part of the bargain according to **1 Samuel 1:27–28**?

This, to me, is amazing! Hannah wanted a child desperately but then she was willing to give him to the Lord "for his whole life." Wow. Although if you really think about it, don't all our children belong to the Lord? Still, her decision was pretty remarkable.

4. What was the result of Hannah "giving" Samuel to the Lord according to?

1 Samuel 2:21

1 Samuel 3:19–21

Up unto this point in time the Israelites were governed by God himself. Unlike their many neighbors they did not have a king. However, just like many of us today, even though what we already have may be great, we still want what the other guy has. So it was with Israel. They wanted a king.

5. What is the name of the new king and why did God allow this change, according to **1 Samuel 9:15–17**?

6. Read **1 Samuel 10:17–19**; what is God's reaction to His people wanting a king and what are your thoughts on this?

Unfortunately, Saul did not last long as king, as he did not follow God as he should. So (and I promise I'm getting to Solomon), Samuel was asked by God to find a new king. This new king was the son of a man named Jesse. Jesse had eight sons, of which David (the man who would be king) was the youngest.

7. Is it surprising to you that God would choose the youngest son (David) versus the oldest (especially if you consider the culture during Old Testament times)?

8. What does His choosing David tell you about God?

9. And finally, what do we learn in **2 Samuel 12:24** and in **1 Kings 1:28–30**?

See, I told you we would get to Solomon!

10. What do we learn about Solomon from **1 Kings 3:7–13**?

11. What lessons can you learn from Solomon?

12. How do the words of **James 3:13–17** tie into the previous two questions?

13. What else do we learn about wisdom in **James 1:5**?

14. What, in your opinion, is the difference between godly wisdom and earthly knowledge?

15. Which of the two do you think is more important and why?

At this point you may be thinking, *What does any of this have to do with our study of the book of Ecclesiastes?* It's a fair question. The answer is manifold. First, I believe it is important to know some basic biblical facts and background if we are going to understand our book's author and what he brings to the table as far as his personal perspective is concerned. In addition, if you haven't read much of the Old Testament, I hope these few scriptures will whet your appetite to read some of the wonderful biblical history that can be found in these often less-read books.

Also, since we don't always get to see how the decisions we make today (good or bad) play out in the future, I thought you might be encouraged by Hannah's story. Hannah, who obediently chose to return her child (Samuel) to God, to thank Him for giving her that child, might not have lived long enough to see all the ways God blessed Samuel. However, because of her obedience and her thankfulness, her son was given the privilege of crowning Israel's first two kings, and he walked with God all his days. (Plus, Hannah was given more children.) Therefore, keep in mind, your obedience and/or thankfulness today may have long-term (even eternal) implications (whether you see them in this life or not). Of course, your disobedience may have long-term (even eternal) consequences as well (whether you experience them in this life or not). Keep in mind, though, "If we confess our sins, he is faithful and just and will forgive us our sins and purify us from all unrighteousness." **(I John 1:9, NIV)**

And finally, I want you to:

grasp the importance of godly wisdom.
appreciate the need to ask for godly wisdom.
understand how applying godly wisdom during this study
(and beyond) will be vital.

As you may have already guessed, this book is no "cake walk"!

All right, now that we have a little background on Solomon (and Samuel), let's return to the first two chapters of Ecclesiastes.

16. As we read these first two chapters, it seems as though Solomon has lived a fairly long life. How do you think being of an older age might affect one's perspective on life?

17. What in your life do you see differently than you did ten years ago? Twenty years ago?

18. Reflect again on the question about God choosing David, the youngest son of Jesse, to be king. Can you see any advantage(s) in David's youth?

19. Do you think movies with titles such as **Grumpy Old Men** are an accurate reflection on what happens to us as we age? Why or why not?

Do you remember the movie **City Slickers**? Do you remember the scene in which Billy Crystal's character, Mitch, addresses the children in his son's grade-school class with these words?

"Value this time in your life, kids, because this is the time in your life when you still have your choices. It goes by so fast.

When you're a teenager, you think you can do anything and you do. Your twenties are a blur.

Thirties you raise your family, you make a little money, and you think to yourself, *What happened to my twenties?*

Forties, you grow a little pot belly, you grow another chin. The music starts to get too loud, one of your old girlfriends from high school becomes a grandmother. Fifties, you have a minor surgery—you'll call it a procedure, but it's a surgery.

Sixties, you'll have a major surgery, the music is still loud, but it doesn't matter because you can't hear it anyway. Seventies, you and the wife retire to Fort Lauderdale. You start eating dinner at 2:00 in the afternoon, you have lunch around 10:00, breakfast the night before, spend most of your time wandering around malls looking for the ultimate soft yogurt and muttering, 'How come the kids don't call? How come the kids don't call?'

The eighties, you'll have a major stroke, and you end up
babbling with some Jamaican nurse who your wife can't stand,
but who you call mama.
Any questions?" [1]

These are pretty funny words coming from a very funny guy who, in
the movie, is going through a midlife crisis. So, it makes me wonder if
Solomon was thinking something similar, if he was going through some
sort of a midlife crisis. More importantly, I'm wondering if Mitch's words
summarize some of your thoughts as well.

20. However, what does **Job 12:12** say regarding aging?

21. Does this change your answer to question 19?

22. Compare what you have learned so far about Solomon as a young
man (according to the previously read verses, **1 Kings 3:7–10**) to
what is written about him when he was older in **1 Kings 11:1–8**.

23. How then would you relate these changes in Solomon to his
being "grumpy"?

Solomon was grumpy because he was missing the point (and maybe
because he was trying to keep so many wives happy!). When he was young
he got off to a good start. He recognized the fact that he was naïve and

needed help. God loved him and he loved God. He sought wisdom over everything else and, thus, when Solomon <u>walked **with** God</u> he had true wisdom (and dare I say, meaning in his life). As he got older, though, he <u>turned **from** God</u> and tried to find fulfillment (or meaning) in everything from earthly knowledge to carnal pleasure, to money. As Dr. Phil would say, "How's that working for you?"

24. How was that working for him, according to the very last sentence of **Ecclesiastes chapter 2**?

25. What is Solomon's particular frustration in **Ecclesiastes 2:17–19**?

26. Yet, how does **1 Kings 2:1–4** and **1 Kings 11:9–13** address Solomon's frustration?

Do you understand that Solomon was dealing with an "**if/then**" situation? When his father, David, transferred the crown to Solomon he made it very clear that **IF** Solomon continued to follow God as David had, **THEN** their "line" (their descendants) would remain on the thrown. However, as noted earlier, while Solomon started on the right path he soon lost his footing and turned from God, His commandments, and, therefore, His blessings.

This is one of the reasons I believe that Solomon was indeed the author of this book. It seems quite clear that he knew someone other than one of his heirs would inherit the throne (and his possessions) because his father (David) had warned him of this many years earlier. And yet, while it was of his own doing he was frustrated.

27. Have you ever "lost your footing," disobeyed God, and then were forced to deal with the consequences?

28. Were you surprised or frustrated, as if God's word somehow didn't apply to you? (Maybe that was Solomon's thought, too.)

29. Yet, what can we learn from **Isaiah 48:17–18**?

30. There was another frustration with which Solomon wrestled. What is it according to **Ecclesiastes 1:11 and 2:16a**?

31. How do you view Solomon's concern (about being remembered) in light of the following verses?

    Psalm 25:6–7

    Hebrews 8:12

    Revelation 3:5

Unless you are a descendant of someone quite famous (or infamous), it is unlikely that you know much about your grandparents' parents.

Even if you do know the names of those a generation or so before you, you undoubtedly don't know much about who they really were—their likes/dislikes, quirks, sense of humor, etc. So, Solomon's comments are accurate.

However, in light of the previous scriptures, this should not concern us. If we trust in Christ as our savior, He will remember us. And it won't be a casual "Hey, you look familiar" remembrance, either. He will remember our name and acknowledge our name before God and His angels, but He will forget our sins! It doesn't get any better than that!

God will **remember our names,** but **forget our sins!**
Woo-hoo!

Two Bright Spots

With all his moaning and complaining (which we'll talk more about later in this study), there were times when Solomon recognized God's goodness and offers of hope.

32. What are your thoughts on these verses?

Ecclesiastes 2:13

Ecclesiastes 2:24–25

Thankfully, it seems Solomon recognized (to some degree, anyway) that **it wasn't life that was meaningless**—it was **life without God that was meaningless.** When I mentioned before that Solomon was missing the point—this is the point:

Life without God is meaningless!

So, what about you? Are you struggling with the meaning of life? Do you view midlife as a time of crisis? Are you getting older and starting to wonder if you will be forgotten? Perhaps you have gotten wrapped up in only what this world has to offer? If so, reflect on the following lines from a wonderful old hymn:

TURN YOUR EYES UPON JESUS,
LOOK FULL IN HIS WONDERFUL FACE,
AND THE THINGS OF EARTH WILL GROW STRANGELY DIM
IN THE LIGHT OF HIS GLORY AND GRACE. [2]

How to Find Meaning in a Meaningless Life

Lesson One

When we get bogged down in the meaninglessness of life here on earth, consider the fact that our time here is brief. <u>Eternity is forever.</u>

Instead of focusing on things like how much stuff we have, or who's going to get "our" stuff, or the fact that we are getting old and frail (and maybe grumpy) and that no one will remember us, focus instead on things above—on Jesus! Find meaning in a God who knows you by name!

> **"Therefore, we do not lose heart. Though outwardly we are wasting away, yet inwardly we are being renewed day by day. For our light and momentary troubles are achieving for us an eternal glory that far outweighs them all. So, we fix our eyes not on what is seen, but on what is unseen. For what is seen is temporary, but what is unseen is eternal."**
>
> (2 CORINTHIANS 4:16–18)

Let's Pray – Dear God, it is almost unbelievable that with all the people throughout the world You know <u>me</u> by name. When I get caught up in the trivialities of this world remind me of that fact and the fact that I will spend eternity with You! Thank you, Jesus! Amen.

WEEK TWO

CHASING AFTER
THE WIND

ECCLESIASTES
CHAPTERS 3 AND 4

As noted in last week's study and the last line of chapter 2, Solomon lamented that after all of his hard work and wealth accumulation, which would end up in the hands of who knows who, he felt as though he had been "chasing after the wind." In fact, he made this statement again and again throughout Ecclesiastes. Of course, this distressed him because, as we all know, you can chase after the wind until the cows come home, but you will never catch it.

Perhaps you feel like this sometimes. Why do you work so hard? Why do you care about putting a healthy meal on the table? Why do you save for retirement? Why do you exercise? Why do you run yourself ragged after those crazy kids? You get the point, why are you chasing after the wind?

Well, a little later in this week's study we're going to address this question. Before we do, however, let's look closely at the first fourteen verses of chapter 3.

Reread Chapter 3:1–14.

If you are of a certain age, you will remember a song that was adopted from the first eight verses of this Ecclesiastes passage. The song to which I'm referring is, "Turn! Turn! Turn! (to Everything There Is a Season)," written by Pete Seeger and recorded by the Byrds way back in the early

1960s.(3) The lyrics to this song, except for the title and the final two lines, were adapted word for word from the English version of this Old Testament book.

I find it a little difficult to believe that a song from the Bible was as popular as this one was during the turbulent 60s, but on the other hand, I would be surprised if many people recognized the words of this song as coming from the Old Testament. Yet what isn't surprising, and is often the case, God's word speaks to all cultures, all generations, and all people whether or not they know it to be the source of what they believe, value, quote, or sing.

1. Which of these eight verses (chapter 3:1–8) is particularly relevant to you as you are working on this study? Why?

2. Do you believe there is a "time for everything"? Why or why not?

3. How is time relevant in these verses?

John 2:4

John 17:1

Romans 9:9

2 Peter 3:8

4. How might the previous verses challenge your thoughts about "time"?

5. How might these same verses encourage you if you are waiting for an answer to a prayer?

6. Speaking of time, what do you think Solomon meant by "He has made everything beautiful in its time"? (verse 11a)

7. Last week we talked a little bit about eternity. What do you think Solomon meant when he said that God has "set eternity in the hearts of men..."?

8. Do you think God has set eternity in the hearts of ALL men and women? Explain.

9. Do you see a link between the first and second parts of verse 11?

10. Continuing with the eternity theme, skip down to verse 14 where we learn that "everything God does will endure forever..." What

is God's purpose (according to this verse) in allowing what He does to last?

11. In answering the previous question your Bible may say that God does this "so mankind will <u>revere</u> Him," or it might say "so mankind may <u>fear</u> Him." What are your first thoughts when you hear the word *fear*?

12. Do you believe that your interpretation of *fear* is how God wants us to approach Him?

Most of us think of being scared or feeling threatened when we hear the word *fear*; perhaps cowering even comes to mind. That is not, I repeat, **NOT** the way God wants us to react to Him! While we certainly must take God seriously, we need to view this word *fear* the way it was translated in more ancient times:

To stand in awe of, to revere, to venerate or respect
(That is the reason why many translations use the word "revere" instead of "fear" in verse 14.)

People today do neither all too often. They are neither afraid of God nor do they respect, revere, or stand in awe of Him. Yet, as the verse below so clearly points out, without a healthy reverence to God we cannot obtain true wisdom. We may be as "smart as a whip," but we will not be wise.

ECCLESIASTES CHAPTERS 3 AND 4

"The fear of the LORD is the beginning of wisdom,
and knowledge of the Holy One is understanding."
(PROVERBS 9:10, NIV)

13. As we concluded last week's study, Solomon gave us some
    positive words to consider in **Ecclesiastes 2:13**. How do you
    equate the first part of that verse to the Proverbs verse above?

14. The second part of the **Proverbs 9:10** verse states that
    "knowledge of the Holy One is understanding." What do you
    think that means?

I imagine you have heard of the apostle Paul. However, I don't know
how familiar you are with his life, especially his life before writing all of
the great books/letters in the New Testament. Suffice it to say, though,
that Paul (initially known as Saul, before his encounter with Christ) "had
it going on." He was a Jew, from a devout Jewish family, and apparently
was a citizen of Rome. He studied under the most noted rabbi of his
time, Gamaliel, and thus quite likely mastered such disciplines as clas-
sical literature and philosophy. He had an incredible comprehension, as
far as memorization is concerned, of Old Testament scripture. (Keep in
mind that was the only testament available back then.) And he had tre-
mendous respect and power within the Jewish community. And yet with
all of his knowledge, all of his learning, and all of his power he lacked
"understanding."

15. Read **Matthew 13:13–15**. How do these verses relate to the apostle Paul and help you better understand the previous question?

You see, Paul's heart was calloused. In fact, his heart was calloused to the point where "though seeing, he could not see, though hearing, he could not hear or understand." His heart was so calloused that while he knew the Old Testament inside and out he didn't recognize the Messiah of which it foretold and even went so far as to persecute those who believed in this Messiah, the Lord Jesus Christ.

16. Look up **Acts 9:1–12**. What was Ananias to do according to the last verse? Why?

So, how was Paul's life turned around to the point of not only believing that Jesus was the Messiah, but to being persecuted himself for that belief? Through Divine revelation, through a newfound reverence for God, he went from simple "head knowledge" to true wisdom and understanding. He understood with his heart and was "healed."

17. What further insight do you get from **1 John 5:20**?

Wisdom and understanding are key to our finding meaning in life. "The fear of the LORD is the beginning of wisdom..." and, as our previous question revealed, it is Jesus Christ who has given us (just as He gave Paul) understanding. One of the most critical things Jesus wants us to understand, to grasp, is truth. But what is truth?

Interestingly, on the cover of *Time* magazine (April 3, 2017 issue) was a question: "Is Truth Dead?" While *Time*'s question had nothing to do with what Jesus is revealing, it is disheartening to find that many today are asking the same question. Is truth dead? The answer, of course, is "no." Even though some in society believe in a "relative truth," one that is subject to their personal perspectives, the truth that Jesus reveals is neither relative nor dead—it is absolute.

18. What "absolute" truth does Jesus reveal in **John 14:6**?

Notice that Jesus doesn't say, "I will show you the truth" or "I will lead you to the truth" or even "I will explain truth to you." What He says is, "**I am the truth.**" Did you catch the fact that Jesus says, "I AM"? Just as God told Moses to tell the Israelites that "I AM" sent him (see **Exodus 3:14**), Jesus also states that He is "I AM." And He not only declares this here in **John**, but in many other places in the New Testament, confirming once again that God and Jesus are one. Therefore, what makes this truth "absolute" is that Jesus says it. So, while some say there are many ways to Heaven, if you believe in the Bible and believe Jesus, then you would be calling Him a liar if you agree with them. **DO NOT MISS THIS!**

> Either Jesus is telling us the truth (and is Truth)
> or He is lying—it can't be both!

19. What additional encouragement does Jesus share with regard to our knowing (and believing) that truth in **John 8:32**?

When we strive for the temporal things of this world—be it success, money, beauty, power, popularity, or possessions—we do so out of ignorance. We don't understand. Having those things don't free us;

they enslave us. As Solomon pointed out in Ecclesiastes 4:8b "…His eyes are not content with his wealth." If we are looking to achieve a sense of freedom by obtaining such things, it will never happen because we will always want more of them. However, Jesus tells us we don't need any of these things. We just need Him! If we know Him—aka truth—He will set us free! (Can I get an amen?)

> THEN YOU WILL KNOW THE TRUTH,
> AND THE TRUTH WILL SET YOU FREE.
>
> (JOHN 8:32, NIV)

Chasing after money, success, etc., is like "chasing after the wind," the title of this week's lesson. I have given it this title even though Solomon only used this phrase twice in this week's lesson, in verses 4:4 and 4:16. (Although we saw it last week, we'll see it pop up in other chapters.) However, I wanted to address this topic because I can see how this sort of thought process could lend itself to meaningless feelings. And because, sadly, Solomon seemed to be "chasing after the wind" throughout this entire chapter, if not the entire book. He was looking for life's answers in the temporal, not the eternal. And he was not getting the answers he wanted.

There is an old Western song called "Tumbling Tumbleweed." The words to this song talk about the lonely life of a cowboy. They try to romanticize this loneliness by saying how free a cowboy may be. But the sad truth is that loneliness is not freeing, it is heartbreaking. It is not at all what God intended for his people. God wants us to experience joy, complete and utter joy! However, if we *chase after the wind* or as we drift through life like tumbleweeds, our lives will be meaningless.

While these words are intended to romanticize the life of a cowboy, if you look at them closely you'll see the sad truth. Loneliness is not freeing, it is heartbreaking. It is not at all what God intended for his people. God wants us to experience joy, complete and utter joy! However, if we *chase after the wind* or, as this song suggests, "drift along like tumbling tumble weeds" our lives will be meaningless.

20. What specific "life questions" did Solomon struggle with in these verses from **Ecclesiastes**?

    a. 3:16–17

    b. 3:18–21

    c. 4:7–12

21. How do the following verses address the previous "life questions" and give us hope/meaning?

    Matthew 25:46

    1 Corinthians 15:42–44

    John 15:5

    Matthew 28:20b

Yes, God will judge the wicked and the righteous,
but the righteous will inherit eternal life.
Yes, both mankind and the animals return to the dust,

but those in Christ will be raised imperishable, in glory and
power, and in new spiritual bodies!
Yes, indeed, it is not for us to be alone. In fact, we can do little
without help, but God will not only help us,
He will be with us—always!
We are bonded by a three-stranded cord—Father, Son, and
Holy Spirit—
and that bond will not be broken!

22. I think **Ecclesiastes 4:13** sums up the entire reason for Solomon's lament. How would you tie this verse to **1 Kings 2:3** (which we looked at last week)?

Solomon accurately stated that it is better to be young and wise than old and foolish, especially if you aren't willing to heed a warning (like the one his father, David, gave him). Similarly, when we don't heed God's warnings—His loving yet cautionary warnings—we, too, can feel as though we are simply going through the motions, or "chasing after the wind," in our own lives.

Did you know that the Hebrew word for "wind" is *ruach*? As is often the case with Hebrew words, this word has another meaning. It can also mean "spirit." Hmmm.

23. What does **John 4:24** tell us?

Wow! This is awesome. **God is Spirit**! Plus, we are reminded that we are to **worship God** in **Spirit** and in **Truth**, "absolute" truth (not relative truth), because truth, as we learned earlier, comes from knowing and believing in Jesus Christ.

Thus, we can follow Solomon's sad example of "wind chasing," where we find ourselves being tossed to and fro with the cares and concerns of this world (which is meaningless). Or we can quit chasing the wind and, instead, chase after God's Spirit, allowing the wind of God's Spirit to lift us. Too often the "kites" of our lives never get airborne, or they get tangled in trees and power lines. However, if we allow ourselves to be lifted by God's Spirit, the "kites" of our lives will soar—and they will soar high and free!

We can chase after the wind, or we can chase after the Spirit!
Which one are you chasing?

How to Find Meaning in a Meaningless Life

Lesson Two

Once again, we see the importance of looking toward eternity. We must understand that no matter what we go through here on earth, it will only last for a time, a season, and then it will pass. We need to quit chasing after the wind (the temporal things of this life) and chase after God. Because chasing after God not only takes the meaninglessness out of life, it will lead us on a high-flying adventure!

> **"But those who trust in the LORD will find new strength. They will soar high on wings like eagles. They will run and not grow weary. They will walk and not faint."**
> (ISAIAH 40:31, NLT)

Let's Pray – Dear God, why do I chase after the silly things in life? Why do I try to fly by my own power? I should know by now that I will get all tangled up if I rely on earthly breezes and my own efforts. You have set eternity in my heart for a purpose. Lift me up, closer to You; far above the mundane, above the ordinary, to the Heavenly realms, where my spirit can soar. Guide me, God, as I seek to worship you in Spirit and in Truth, and help me fly! In Jesus' name, amen.

WEEK THREE

BEING QUIET AND CONTENT

ECCLESIASTES
CHAPTERS 5 AND 6

"Guard your steps when you go to the house of God." Stated another way: "Walk softly when you come into God's presence." What a great way to start this week's lesson!

Reread **verses 1–7 of chapter 5.**

1. What would you say are the main themes in these verses?

In looking at these verses I see "being quiet" as the main theme here (although there are certainly other, more subtle ones).

2. A verse with which you may be familiar is **Psalm 46:10**. What does this verse say?

3. How would you compare the above verse and verse 2 of chapter 5?

4. List several reasons why you believe it is good to be still/quiet.

5. Is being still/quiet something at which you excel? Why or why not?

6. Can you think of a time when you argued with someone when you didn't fully understand the facts of the matter?

7. How did it make you feel when you realized your opinions were misguided?

8. Look at **Job 38:1–11**. How do these verses relate to the previous question?

In the first part of this passage from **Job**, God says, "Who is this that darkens my counsel with words without knowledge?" It is as if God is saying (perhaps a little tongue in cheek), "Seriously, you are questioning the Creator of the universe?"

9. In fact, what is Job's response to God in **Job 42:1–3**? (Pay special attention to the second part of this reading.)

I can't tell you the number of times I have been adamant about something and fully believed my stance was correct, only to discover at some point how wrong I was. Perhaps you can relate. In God's answer to Job He gave not only Job, but all of us an idea of why we should be still most of the time and come to terms with the fact that God is God and we are not!

If you continue to read the rest of **Job** you will see that God has a command of things that we, just like Job, can't even begin to understand.

In the previous weeks we learned that a lot of Solomon's problems, a lot of his frustrations, were because he chose not to listen to God. However, what do we learn from the following two verses?

Psalm 81:13–14

John 15:9–11

Are you seeing a pattern here? God wants us to listen. Of course, listening doesn't mean that we simply hear what God has to say and then continue to do whatever we want. With listening comes obedience. If you are like me, though, perhaps you struggle with the word obedience. We equate it to a harsh overlord telling us to jump and expecting us to say, "How high?" But the obedience that God requires doesn't come from a position of power, it comes from a heart of love. God wants to protect us from our enemies. He wants to guard us from hurt and He wants us to experience joy! God knows what is best for us and wants us to love Him enough that we truly believe it.

Think of the many parents who beg their children not to get involved with drugs. The parents aren't trying to squash their children's fun, but rather they are hoping to protect them from pain or even death. Parents love their children. Yet, like each of us, the child can appreciate the parents' love and avoid drugs, or they can "hear" what the parents say but refuse to obey.

10. We are reminded of God's love for us and the reasons we should listen to Him in **Jeremiah 29:11–13**. What do these verses mean to you?

The other theme in these opening verses revolves around vows. While I don't want to spend a lot of time on this I do think it is important to see what is said about making vows in the New Testament.

11. What does Jesus say about vows in **Matthew 5:33–37**?

12. Can you see a tie between the previous verse and one of the Ten Commandments? (See **Exodus 20:7** if you aren't sure.) What's the big deal?

13. This thought is reiterated in **James 5:12**. How does this apply to you/Christians today?

OK, let's switch gears a bit and look at the rest of chapter 5 and all of chapter 6 in a broad-brush/singular-theme fashion. This may be a little difficult because many things are discussed here. However, I want to focus on money, or rather not money per se, but contentment.

Recently my husband and I and another couple went to see the movie *All the Money in the World*. Although not one hundred percent true, it is based on facts taken from the life of J. Paul Getty and the real-life kidnapping of his grandson, J. Paul Getty III (Paul), the ransom for whom Mr.

Getty refused to pay. While you may not know much about J. Paul Getty, according to the Guinness Book of Records, he was the world's richest private citizen in 1966. He had an estimated worth of $1.2 billion, which, based on simple inflation, would be worth well over $9 billion in today's dollars. Using a seven percent return rate, that amount would be valued at over $35 BILLION today!

However, when asked how much money was enough, Mr. Getty reportedly replied, "A little more." Seriously? Yet, while this may seem ridiculous to us, didn't Solomon say the same thing?

14. Look at both verse 10 and verse 13 (of chapter 5). What parallels can you draw between these verses and what you now know about Mr. Getty?

In **1 Timothy 6:10 (NIV)**, we learn that "the love of money is the root of all kinds of evil." Money itself isn't evil, but the love of it is. However, with both Solomon and J. Paul Getty, the question isn't really about having enough money; it is a question of contentment.

15. Abraham Lincoln once said, "Contentment makes poor men rich, discontentment makes rich men poor." What do you think is meant by that statement?

16. Similarly, there is an anonymous comment that states, "Contentment is not the fulfillment of what we want but the appreciation for what we have." What would you say is the difference between this and Lincoln's comment?

17. Look at verse 18 of chapter 5. Would you say satisfaction and contentment are the same?

18. How would you tie the above comments about contentment to verses 19 and 20 of chapter 5?

19. What did Paul say about contentment in **Philippians 4:11–12**?

20. Paul said that he "learned" to be content. How do you think one "learns" contentment?

Contentment is a tricky thing. We often find ourselves content until someone comes along and tells us or shows us why we shouldn't be content. Isn't that what advertising is all about? You may be perfectly content with your five-year-old car until some advertiser tells you that you deserve one that is a little more sleek or shiny, or that goes a little faster. You may be content saving some money by taking a stay-at-home vacation until your Facebook "friend" shares pictures of her family parasailing off some tropical beach.

21. Look up **Exodus 20:17** and explain how this scripture relates to contentment.

22. To covet generally means to want (perhaps strongly) what someone else has, but can you see how comparing ourselves to others can also be a form of coveting?

23. Do you ever compare yourself to others and thus focus more on what you <u>don't</u> have (compared to them) rather than what you <u>do</u> have?

For you it may not be money; it may be the things you have or have not accomplished. You compare yourself to others and become discontent when you feel as though you don't measure up.

24. What does **John 12:42–43** say in this regard?

I can't speak for you but, sadly, I have to admit that at times I, too, have loved the praise of men more than the praise of God. I was reminded how shallow that thinking is when I read the closing lines of my friend Dawn's Christmas letter. In it she wrote this: "It's easy for us to place an emphasis on accomplishments to bring meaning and value to life, but a problem occurs when we don't succeed. Thankfully, our value isn't based on performance. I hope we can all recognize the great gift of grace we have in Jesus, who sees our worth and came to provide love, joy, and peace."

I found her words both convicting and encouraging. She is right; we don't have to accomplish something in order to bring meaning to our lives because, more often than not, our efforts are to please someone else, not ourselves and certainly not God. We want to succeed to show others how wonderful we are. But what if we don't succeed or if others don't appreciate our accomplishments? Thankfully our value does not rest in the opinion of others. Our value is found in Christ Jesus and it isn't based on performance; it is based on His love and His grace, His Great Gift of Grace, as He presents us blameless and righteous before God. Amazing, isn't it?

25. Do you think there is a link between contentment and gratitude? If so, how?

Have you ever given a wonderful gift to someone about whom you care deeply? Perhaps it was a gift you searched high and low for, or maybe you spent far too much money on the gift, but you wanted to see the joy on their face when they opened it. Have you ever done such a loving thing only to have the recipient toss the gift aside or, even worse, complain about it? Was it a horrible gift? Were you a horrible gift-giver? Or was the recipient simply ungrateful?

God has given us His Great Gift of Grace and all too often we toss it aside or complain about it!

26. What do we learn from these verses?

   Psalm 9:1–2

   Psalm 103:1–2

   Psalm 118:28–29

   Philippians 4:4

27. Let's go one step further and look at **Psalm 95:1–6**. Write these verses below and then underline the various ways in which we can worship God.

> "What day is it?" asked Winnie the Pooh.
> "It's today," squeaked Piglet.
> "My favorite day," said Pooh. (4)

**Oh, that we could be as content as Pooh and thank God,
every day, for today!**

How to Find Meaning in a Meaningless Life

Lesson Three

Be still before our God and remember His great love for you. Obey Him because you love Him and know the plans He has for you to prosper, not harm you. And as you pray and study, His word will let His still, soft voice quiet your soul and give you peace.

With peace comes contentment. Think of all the many blessing you have and thank God for them—often. Do not seek the approval of others or compare yourself with those around you and what they "seemingly" have.

> **"But seek first his kingdom and his righteousness, and all these things will be given to you as well."**
> (MATTHEW 6:33, NIV)

Let's Pray – Father God, sometimes I look to others to give me my self-worth, others whose praise is often misguided and fleeting. Help me remember that you alone are the only one whom I should seek to please and that you love me unconditionally. In Jesus' name, Amen.

WHEN LIFE SEEMS OFF BALANCE

ECCLESIASTES
CHAPTERS 7 AND 8

While, as mentioned before, I find the entire book of Ecclesiastes to be a little strange, I find these two chapters to be the most peculiar. Not only did Solomon seem to go back and forth between what is right and what is wrong, sometimes calling good, bad, and bad, good, he himself seemed a little off balance. Thus, the reason why I have entitled this week's lesson: *When Life Seems Off Balance.*

Let's start by looking at a few of Solomon's opening comparisons in chapter 7. Explain your response as to whether you agree or disagree.

1. A good name is better than fine perfume. Agree or disagree?

2. The day of your death is better than the day of your birth. Agree or disagree?

3. A house of mourning is better than a house of feasting. Agree or disagree?

4. Sorrow is better than laughter. Agree or disagree?

5. A sad face is good for the heart. Agree or disagree?

I would agree that a good name is better than fine perfume. That certainly makes sense. I could also agree, particularly for those of us who have placed our faith in Jesus Christ, how the day of our death might be better than the day of our birth. I mean, no matter your age, would you really enjoy starting all over again, especially when you know Heaven awaits you sooner now than it did on the day you were born? So I can appreciate the sentiment here, too. However, I strongly disagree with Solomon's statements about mourning, sorrow, and a sad face. While we have learned previously in this study that there are times for such things, who wants to go through life like that?

6. Read **Luke 10:21**. What does the <u>first line</u> tell us about how Jesus was feeling?

7. Why was Jesus in such a mood?

8. Since we have been discussing wisdom throughout this study, can you see the difference between the *wise and learned* mentioned in the above verse from Luke's gospel and those who have *godly wisdom*?

9. Do you think God, based on this passage, has a sense of humor when it comes to those with earthly knowledge? Explain.

10. What is Jesus' desire for us, according to **John 15:11**?

Do you see what I am saying about Solomon being a little *off*? If Jesus wants us to be joyful, why on earth would Solomon say that sorrow and sadness are good?

11. Of course, you might be thinking that Jesus wasn't born yet; however, what do we learn about Jesus in **John 1:1** and **John 1:14**?

12. As you continue reading **Ecclesiastes 7: 4–9**, I imagine you will agree with much of what Solomon said here. Pick one of the six verses and expound on it.

13. Skip ahead to verse 15. Solomon stated that he had seen both the righteous perish and the wicked live a long time. What similar thought did he mention in chapter 8:14?

14. I think Solomon has a point here, and I have to admit it does seem unfair. How then do we come to terms with such injustices when things in life seem unfair?

15. What insight might you gather from the second part of **Matthew 5:45b**?

How many times have you heard your kids holler, "That isn't fair"? To which you might have replied, "You know what? Life isn't fair." And you would be right. Life isn't fair. In fact, I would even say that God isn't fair. Don't misunderstand, God is just, but He isn't necessarily fair. (Bear with me if you are bothered by this statement. We will discuss it further in just a bit.) That is why both good people and bad people get to enjoy the sunshine and why it rains on the righteous and the unrighteous alike. That is why sometimes the "good" die young. That is why some criminals get away with murder and sometimes innocent people go to prison for crimes they did not commit. Life, this life, is unfair and Solomon was troubled by that. It seems to have caught him off balance.

16. How could **Romans 8:18** help you maintain your balance when life seems unfair?

17. What further encouragement might you get from **Romans 8:28**?

18. What insight do the following verses provide as to the reason why life here on earth is unfair?

    Romans 16:20a

    Ephesians 2:1–2

    Ephesians 6:12

As these verses reveal, life here on earth is unfair because Satan still maintains a foothold. God has not yet crushed Satan and established His kingdom. But He will.

19. Therefore, what should we keep in mind when this life seems unfair, according to the first part of **Philippians 3:20?**

20. Still I'm thinking some of you may still be reeling a bit from my comment about God not being fair. But do you know how I know God isn't fair? Look at these passages:

    John 3:16

    Romans 5:8

Romans 8:1–2

Titus 3:3–6

Think about it, how fair is it that God loved us, while he hated Him? How fair is it that God's Son had to die for all of the terrible things we have done? Isn't that sort of like you going to prison for an armed robbery that I committed? And you being happy to serve the time because you love me so much! Sorry, to me that is totally unfair, and yet that is how God works. He unfairly blesses us when we should be enduring punishment. He welcomes us into His kingdom when He should be locking the door and throwing away the key. God is wonderfully unfair!

THE QUALITY OF MERCY IS NOT STRAINED;
IT DROPPETH AS THE GENTLE RAIN
FROM HEAVEN UPON THE PLACE BENEATH.
IT IS TWICE BLESSED;
IT BLESSETH HIM THAT GIVES AND HIM THAT TAKES...
IT IS AN ATTRIBUTE OF GOD HIMSELF...
THOUGH JUSTICE BE THY PLEA, CONSIDER THIS,
THAT IN THE COURSE OF JUSTICE,
NONE OF US SHOULD SEE SALVATION...[5]

Let the last few lines of these verses sink in, because they are true. If justice were applied, "none of us should see salvation." Thus, our salvation is completely unfair.

Are you familiar with a piece of exercise equipment called a Bosu? If not, imagine one of those large workout balls cut in half with the flat side resting on the floor; a half dome, if you will. Bosus are used by sports trainers, athletes, and people like me because, among other benefits, it increases our ability to balance, and balance strengthens our core; studies show that a strong core impacts nearly everything we do.

I have to admit, when I first started working out on my Bosu it didn't take much for me to lose my balance. Even closing my eyes would make me wobble. But the more I used it the better I got. Sometimes circumstances in life seem so unfair they cause us to wobble. However, the more we trust God, the more we see how He can take unfair situations and make something good come from them, the less we wobble. He strengthens us down to our very our core and helps us find balance.

21. What do these two verses tell us about handling unfair situations?

   Romans 5:3–5

   James 1:2–4

As these verses explain, it is actually important that we be subjected to unfair situations and/or sufferings if we are going to grow spiritually. None of us like to be treated unfairly or to suffer in any way, but without such experiences our character will come up lacking and we may never have the strength to persevere when things in life get really difficult.

In their workbook, *Experiencing God*, Henry Blackaby and Claude King stated that we are "Created Not for Time, but Eternity." They went on to say:

"God did not create you for time; He created you for eternity. Time (your lifetime on earth) provides the opportunity to get acquainted with Him. It is an opportunity for Him to develop your character in His likeness. Then eternity will have its fullest dimensions for you.

   "If you just live for time (the here and now), you will miss the ultimate purpose of creation. If you live for time, you will allow your past to mold and shape your life today. Your life as a child of God ought to be shaped

by the future (what you will be one day). God uses your present time to
mold and shape your future usefulness here on earth and in eternity." (6)

22. In the previous question, you read (in **James 1:4**) that we are to
    persevere "so that you may be mature and complete, not lacking
    anything." What do you think that statement means and how can
    you relate it to the above quote?

23. While it may be difficult to acknowledge, what areas of your
    character do you see as lacking?

24. Can you think of a recent time when God used some situation to
    strengthen this aspect of your character?

25. Go back to **Ecclesiastes 8:2–4**. Keeping in mind that Solomon
    was king, do you see any problems with what he was saying
    in these verses, especially as it pertains to what we have been
    discussing? (If this one perplexes you a bit, just move on.)

26. Can you fill in the blanks of this often-quoted statement?
    Power tends to _____ and _____ power
    _____ absolutely.

You may or may not be familiar with this quotation but it was written in a letter by John Emerich Edward Dalberg Acton, the first Baron of Acton (1834–1902), to Bishop Mandell Creighton in 1887. What he wrote was, "Power tends to corrupt, and absolute power corrupts absolutely. Great men are almost always bad."

I don't know if I totally agree with this statement, but I do see how it could be a reflection on Solomon's *imbalance* because, as king, he had power. Thus he told us to "Obey the king's command" and also, "Since the king's word is supreme, who can say to him, 'What are you doing?'"

In Solomon's time, I imagine, as is often the case today, those in power tend to surround themselves with *yes men*, people who simply will not question what their superiors (those in power) are doing. This quite possibly could have contributed to Solomon's downfall. However, if everyone around us agrees with everything we say or do then we, too, need to be careful or the same could lead to our downfall as well.

We get off balance, or are led astray, when we steer clear of God, His word, or those who lovingly remind us that we are going in the wrong direction. We get thrown off course when we take the easy way out, avoid challenges, or fail to take a stand. And our character suffers. As the previous quote from *Experiencing God* reminds us, we do these things because we are more concerned about the here and now than about eternity.

Think about Solomon's life. He started out loving God, listening to God, and obeying God. But then he got some power. And he got so wrapped up in his power that he thought he could simply ignore God's command (to him and all Israelites) not to marry non-Hebrew women.

God gave this command to Solomon, and all of the Israelites, so that they might not be pressured by their wife(s) to jointly worship their wives' gods in conjunction with the one true God, the Lord God Almighty. But as Solomon became more powerful, he ignored God's command and went ahead and married Egyptians, Moabites, Ammonites, Edomites, Sidonians, and Hittites to the tune of seven hundred wives and three hundred concubines!

27. Do you t.hink this might be why Solomon said what he did in **Ecclesiastes 7:28?** (LOL)

28. Do you remember the outcome of Solomon's disobedience? (If not, go back and reread **1 Kings 11:1–13**.)

29. Read **I Corinthians 15:33**. How does this verse relate to both Solomon and to us today with regard to maintaining our balance?

30. According to the verses below, what are we to do to help steady others?

    Luke 17:3

    2 Timothy 4:2

31. And how are we to do it?

32. Does your Bible use the term *rebuke*? What does that word mean to you and how do you see yourself carrying out a rebuke? (Use a dictionary if you like.)

33. Some translations us the word exhort. What does the word *exhort* mean?

34. How and when do you rebuke or exhort others?

35. Do you see the value in both giving and getting rebuked or exhorted?

Ok, let's wrap things up for the week.

36. Read **Ecclesiastes 8:16–17** and note below your thoughts on these two verses.

37. Do you think Solomon was frustrated, resigned, or in awe of the fact that no matter how smart or how wise a person is, he or she can't really comprehend the meaning of all things here on earth?

38. Since we have no idea, really, what Solomon's thoughts were when he wrote these last lines, there is no right or wrong answer. However, what about you? Are you frustrated, resigned, or

in awe of the fact that you really can't fully grasp the meaning of life, this life? (Again, no right or wrong answer.)

While we may not understand the meaning of life here on earth, we can be confident of this:

> For you have been born again, not of perishable seed, but of imperishable, through the living and enduring word of God. For "all men are like the grass and all their glory is like the flowers of the field, The grass withers and the flowers fall, But the word of the Lord stands forever."
> (I PETER 1:23–25, NIV)

How to Find Meaning in a Meaningless Life

Lesson Four

Remember how ***wonderfully unfair*** our God is. Never forget his mercy and goodness.

Develop a strong core that is shaped by the future, not the here and now.

When (this) life seems unfair, maintain your balance by staying in God's word, by obeying God's commandments, and by surrounding yourself with friends who will *call you out* when you start to wobble.

> **"Then you will no longer be infants, tossed back and forth by the waves and blown here and there by every wind of teaching and by the cunning and craftiness of men in their deceitful scheming."**
>
> (EPHESIANS 4:14, NIV)

Let's Pray – Father God, when I sometimes get wrapped up in the "unfairness" of things, remind me that if you were fair, I would not see salvation. When things shake me, help me maintain my balance. Surround me with people who love me enough to rebuke me, guide me, and encourage me as I make my way in this (sometimes seemingly meaningless) life. In Jesus' name, amen.

SINNERS AND SAINTS

Ecclesiastes
Chapters 9 and 10

Let's look closely at the first three verses of chapter 9.

1. What are your thoughts on verse 1? Do you agree that what happens in our lives is entirely in God's hands?

2. What would you say is the meaning of the phrase "no man knows whether love or hate awaits him"?

3. For the most part, Solomon had a valid point in verse 3 with regard to man's destiny. What is it?

One of the movie theaters I frequent in Pittsburgh has pictures along the wall of the lady's room of legendary, old-Hollywood actors and actresses. People like, Marilyn Monroe, Paul Newman, Elizabeth Taylor, Cary Grant, Audrey Hepburn, Humphrey Bogart, and Marlon Brando. Famous people, beautiful people, dead people. Dead, yes, all dead.

Isn't this Solomon's point? In the end, no matter how famous or infamous, how wonderful or traitorous, how good or how bad, we all die. Unfortunately, this reality seems to taint Solomon's entire view on life but, either consciously or unconsciously, he made some good points.

4. What does verse 4 of chapter 9 tell us?

5. Do you agree with his statement?

6. What did we learn last week about hope in **Romans 5:3–5**?

7. Go back a couple of verses to **Romans 5:1–2**. In what hope should we rejoice?

Amazingly God is glorified by our faith in His grace. In other words, when we take God at His word, His divine purpose, for us to be in a relationship with Him, is accomplished and it brings Him glory.

8. Exactly what is it that we are hoping for, according to **Titus 1:1–2**?

9. Based on these same verses, how can we be certain of this hope?

Do you remember, back in chapter 2, that we determined that Jesus is either telling us the truth or He is lying? The same can be said for God. God is either telling us the truth or He is lying, but as Paul noted, "**God does not lie.**"

10. Why is it that God does not lie, according to **Numbers 23:19?**

11. Who, however, does lie according to **John 8:42–44?**

12. Satan is not only a liar, he is the father of all lies. In fact, what is absolutely missing from his character? (Hint: There is no _____ in him.)

13. Continuing on in chapter 9, what did Solomon suggest in verse 8?

14. How can you relate this verse to **Psalm 51:7** and **Isaiah 1:18?**

15. Look at **Hebrews 1:9.** While the writer was speaking of Jesus, since we are heirs with Jesus, with what kind of oil will we also be anointed? Why?

Solomon spoke of being anointed with oil, but he seemed to be missing the joy. Oh sure, he went on to say that we should enjoy our spouse, whom we love, but then he continued with a summation, once again, of how meaningless life is. Perhaps this is because he had not loved righteousness or hated wickedness. I mean how can one follow after unrighteousness and wickedness (aka sin) and have joy? Following the path of sin may bring temporary pleasure, but it will eventually lead to destruction. Life <u>without</u> sin is a joyful life!

16. Look now at verses 11 and 12. Can you see how his statement that "time and chance happen to them all" is a reflection on his joyless take on life?

Sadly, perhaps, the first part of verse 12 is all too correct: "no man knows when his hour will come." As I am writing this section of the study we have had another school shooting, this time in Florida. This happened while we were all still reeling from the heinous shootings that occurred in Las Vegas. In both cases numerous unsuspecting people, many of whom were quite young, were simply attending school or enjoying a concert, only to be gunned down without any notice or cause. I'm sure none of them went about their day thinking that that day would be their last.

I say sadly "perhaps" because those who have accepted Jesus Christ as their Lord and Savior will continue on to an eternal life in Heaven. We who are left behind may grieve, but they will be rejoicing! But for those who are lost, who do not know Christ as their Savior, there are no words to describe the sadness that will befall them.

You see, that is the main reason I have given this week's chapter the title of *Sinners and Saints*. Because the only difference between the two, since we are all sinners actually, is the difference between accepting the gift of salvation from God or rejecting it. Those who reject God's offer will die in their sin, because they chose not to believe in God or His word.

It's just that simple.
The difference between a sinner and a saint
is the difference between unbelief and belief.

17. **Hebrews 3:19**, while talking literally about those Israelites who did not enter Canaan, is also clearly stating the reason why some will not enter the kingdom of God. What does this verse say?

You see, just as the Old Testament Israelites who failed to believe God's promises were denied entrance into the Promised Land, so will everyone today who fails to believe God's promises be denied entrance into Heaven, God's ultimate Promised Land.

Contrarily, **Romans 10:13 (NIV)** states that "Everyone who calls upon the name of the Lord will be saved." Or stated another way, everyone who believes God's promises will live forever with Him.

18. However, what does **Romans 10:14** prompt us to do?

So true. How can someone believe in Christ if they have never heard of Him? This is why it is so important for us to tell others the good news about Jesus Christ, because they can't believe in Him if they have never really heard about Him. Furthermore, we should not hesitate in telling others because, just like those who have died in random shootings or in car accidents or of a sudden heart attack, we do not know when anyone's hour will come.

Therefore, if a person can't <u>believe</u> without hearing about Christ and the only difference between a sinner and a saint is the difference between <u>unbelief</u> and <u>belief</u>, then we must tell others so they might <u>believe</u>!

If you are a believer in Jesus Christ, you are a saint. In fact in **1 Corinthians 1:2 (NKJV)**, Paul reminded us that we are all called to be saints when he wrote "To the church of God that is in Corinth, to those sanctified in Christ Jesus, called to be saints together with all those who in every place call upon the name of our Lord Jesus Christ, both their Lord and ours..."

Depending on your faith background, however, you may understandably be surprised to learn that we are all saints, but the scriptures (a few of which we'll look at shortly) are quite clear. All believers (who call upon the name of our Lord Jesus Christ) are saints.

To better explain this let's look at a passage from the book *Liturgy of the Ordinary* by Tish Harrison Warren. In writing about the Protestant Reformation, Tish said:

"It (the Protestant Reformation) was understood 'as a conflict about doctrine...' And it was. But what captured the imagination of the commoner in Europe during the Reformation was not only the finer points of doctrine, but the earthy notion of vocation... The Reformers taught that a farmer may worship God by being a good farmer and that a parent changing diapers could be as near to Jesus as the pope. This was scandal." [7]

When you first hear this statement, you may think it is scandalous, too, but (and mind you I don't mean any disrespect) the pope may be pope because of his dedication to God and his election to that position. But he, too, is a sinner like you and me, and had to accept God's gift of salvation just as we have.

And while many former popes have been canonized by the Church as saints, they were every bit as human as we are. Today we may recognize the pope because of his papal robes, but underneath beats the same kind of repentant heart as that which beats in believing farmers or mothers or doctors or teachers.

As Paul reminded us:

"You are all sons of God through faith in Christ Jesus, There is neither Jew nor Greek, slave nor free, male or female; for you are all one in Christ Jesus"

(GALATIANS 3:26 AND 28, NKJV)

19. What do these verses tell us about saints?

    1 Samuel 2:9a

    Psalm 30:4

    Psalm 149:4–5

    Ephesians 1:15–18

I hope these verses help you appreciate the fact that you (if you are a believer in Jesus Christ) are a saint! Okay, moving on…

20. Let's wrap up chapter 9 by looking at verse 17 and 18. What are your thoughts on verse 17?

21. How might you tie Solomon's comment in verse 18, that "one sinner destroys much good," to **I Corinthians 15:33** that we studied last week?

22. Now read <u>all</u> of chapter 10. What are your thoughts as you go over these verses?

The first thing that came to my mind as I read chapter 10 was how much these verses parallel those of Proverbs. Turn back to just about any chapter in Proverbs and you'll see what I mean. The layout is virtually the same and the quips are quite similar; a contrast between good and bad or wise and foolish. These verses in chapter 10, similarly, are all rather commonsense thoughts arranged much like those in the book of Proverbs. I mention this only as another indication of the likelihood of Solomon being the author of the book we have been studying.

23. Pick any one of the verses from chapter 10 (other than verses 19 and 20) and explain in your own words what you believe it means.

24. Verse 19 concludes with "but money is the answer to everything." Commentaries give several explanations to what these words might mean. However, without looking at any commentary, what are your thoughts on this comment?

25. Finally, what wisdom can you take from verse 20?

I'm not sure that a warning regarding gossip or being careful about who you tell what applies to things that give life meaning, but still, its good advice.

How to Find Meaning in a Meaningless Life

Lesson Five

Remember, you are a saint! This isn't because of the good things you have done but simply because you have put your faith in the promises of God.

Know for certain that the hope you place in Jesus Christ will not disappoint you, because God does not lie.

Come to terms with the fact that you will die (physically), but if you have placed your faith in Jesus Christ, you will live forever.

> **"When the perishable has been clothed with the imperishable, and the mortal with immortality, then the saying that is written will come true: 'Death has been swallowed up in victory. Where, O death, is your victory? Where, O death, is your sting?'"**
>
> (1 CORINTHIANS 15:54–55, NIV)

Let's Pray – Dear Lord, because of your son's sacrifice I am a joint heir with Jesus, a friend of the almighty God and a saint! Help me to remember these truths and to live a life that is reflective of them and glorifies you. I praise you today for the certainty of life eternal so that I, too, can say with confidence: Death, where is your victory? Death, where is your sting? In Jesus' name, amen.

THE MAKER OF ALL THINGS

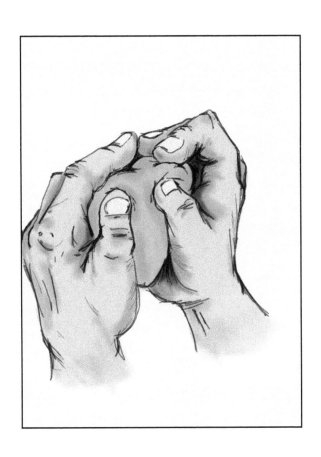

Ecclesiastes
Chapters 11 and 12

Let's begin this week by focusing first on chapter 11. As you can see, this chapter (and much of chapter 12) is very much like chapter 10 from last week, wherein Solomon was offering some sort of cleverly disguised practical advice. Cleverly disguised are the operative words this week, as many of these sayings are rather difficult to interpret.

1. Read verses 1 and 2. These two verses may be speaking to financial matters. Can you explain how so?

2. Verse 3 seems self-evident, but verse 4, while speaking literally about farming, has a deeper meaning. What do these words mean to you and how could you apply them to everyday life?

3. As you can tell, verse 5 is where I got this week's title. Do you agree that God is the maker of all things? Why or why not?

4. What does **Hebrews 2:10** say?

5. What two mysteries did Solomon mention in verse 5?

Earlier in this study, when we were coming to terms with the fact that God is God and we are not, we read from the book of **Job** and saw how God challenged Job with regard to His many mysteries. In the following question we see one of Job's friends, Elihu, similarly questioning him.

6. Look at **Job 37:14–18**. Which of these questions do you find most intriguing? Why?

7. Can you think of any reason as to why Solomon mentioned God as being the maker of all things at this point in our reading? (There is no right or wrong answer.)

8. In verses 7 through 10 (of chapter 11), Solomon turned his attention to the younger generation as he offered his advice. Again, what are your thoughts as to why he might be addressing those who are young?

9. Does the first verse in chapter 12 provide any additional clarity regarding the previous question?

The last part of the previous verse says, "before the days of trouble come and the years approach when you will say, 'I find no pleasure in them.'" In these words, we again get the impression that Solomon was advanced in age and, as previously concluded, had become a grumpy old man. Note that while I use the term *grumpy*, I think it might be better to say he was remorseful or disillusioned. Or better still, that he was looking back on his life with regret. And, I believe, this regret stems from the fact that he slowly walked away from the God of his youth.

Interestingly, while the God of his youth gave him the desires of his heart and loved him deeply, Solomon, apparently, at some point in his life, started taking matters into his own hands, disobeyed God, and thereby forfeited the close relationship he once had with the Maker of All Things.

We can make this assumption by considering the admonishing words Solomon used when he asked his readers to remember their Creator in the days of your youth, before they find no pleasure in them. To me, he is looking back with regret on the life he might have had had he continued his close relationship with the Almighty. Still, to his credit, he wanted to make sure his readers don't make the same mistake.

Sometimes it's easy, isn't it? To look back on life and realize where we messed up, where we went wrong, where we perhaps failed to remember our Creator. And when we look back at the mistakes we have made, more often than not we realize that these mistakes come with a price and that price is regret. So it was with Solomon. He was building a bigger and bigger kingdom, getting wealthier, accumulating more and more wives, but somehow he forgot his Creator and was having regrets in the end.

To me, two of the saddest words in the English language are *if only*. *If only* I had listened to my parents, *if only* I had studied harder, *if only* I had saved more, *if only* I taught my children more about God, *if only* I'd taken better care of myself, etc. You get the picture.

1. Do you have an *if only* in your life?

2. Is there any way you can change your *if only*?

Recently I was reading an article about Chris Rock, the comedian, about a new stand-up show he was doing on Netflix. This was the first stand-up show Chris had done in quite a while and the reviewer applauded it. However, it explained that much of this new show was devoted to Chris coming to terms, humorously of course, with how he had messed up his life. You see, as his popularity, wealth, and accolades increased he "forgot his Creator" (he lost his moral compass) and got involved in an extramarital affair that destroyed his eighteen-year marriage and brought much pain to his whole family.

In another article I read on the matter, Chris admitted that he felt he, as the big moneymaker of the family, was entitled to cheat, but then he went on to say, "That actually goes the other way. My faults are magnified. Your significant other, if they really love you, has a high opinion of you. And you let them down."

Talk about regrets! I would venture to guess that this was one big *if only* time in Chris's life.

Fascinatingly, though, Chris concluded the article by adding, "I wanna find some peace, 'cause people usually find that peace in a horrible time. Why does that have to be? Maybe I can find God without being in shambles. Maybe I can reach a higher plain spiritually without being in a near-death experience."(8)

Wow. How insightful. Why do we often wait until our lives are in shambles before we reach out to or return to God? Wouldn't our lives be more peaceful, more meaningful, if we were to reach out to God early in our lives and continued to walk with Him throughout its entirety?

A good friend of mine has a quote by C. S. Lewis at the bottom of her email. It says,

> "You may forget that you are at every moment totally dependent on God."

Think about that statement. Not only is God the Maker of All Things; when push comes to shove, the truth is that we are totally sustained by Him! Therefore, should we not choose to walk closely with Him?

3. Have you ever thought of God as your significant other, the one who really loves you and has a high opinion of you (in the same way Chris Rock thought about his wife)?

4. In light of the previous question, how would this perception of God help keep you from disappointing Him or avoid future *if onlys* in your life?

5. If you have an *if only*, a regret, that relates to God, is it ever too late to make things right?

6. What do these verses say with regard to the previous question?

Psalm 103:12

Malachi 3:7

Romans 8:38–39

1 John 1:9

7. Let's continue on in chapter 12. Read verses 2 through 8. What was the overall condition that Solomon was describing?

8. Pick a couple of these verses and explain what Solomon was specifically depicting in the imagery he used.

9. Now read verses 9 through 12. What are your thoughts about these verses?

10. While in verse 8 Solomon reiterated that life was meaningless, in verses 9 through 12 he seemed to be turning a corner. Can you see beyond the cynicism he expressed throughout much of this book and recognize the hope his words bring? Explain.

11. Read the last few verses in this chapter. What do you think Solomon meant when he said, "Now all has been heard" (verse 13)?

12. Do you agree with his conclusion in the second part of verse 13?

13. Compare Solomon's conclusion to **John 14:21, 23–24**. What additional insight do these verses provide?

14. Verse 14 may cause you pause, but what encouragement does it bring?

Revering God and obeying His commands, because we know they are given out of love, is basically all with which we need to concern ourselves while we make our journey through life. This is our whole purpose, and you may be thinking this sounds too simple. Well it is, and yet it isn't. Obeying God's commands to love one another, spread the good news about His son, walk in His ways, study His word, etc. can be easy to understand, but difficult to execute.

Knowing, too, that those who seemingly get away with evil in this life will be brought to judgement in the next should help us come to terms with life's injustices. But understand that while we remain here on earth, that can be difficult at times as well.

As mentioned in the early part of this study, there is a big difference between being intelligent and having godly wisdom. Godly wisdom is the key to understanding life's meaning and our having a close walk with our creator. Solomon was granted such wisdom. Thus, being the optimist that I am, I like to believe that Solomon, the man to whom God gave this wisdom, wised up in his old age and turned his life back to the one who so richly blessed him.

I can maintain this belief because the Bible doesn't tell us a lot about the last years of Solomon's life. In fact, in speaking of Solomon's death, **1 Kings 11:41–43** (NIV) simply says, "As for the other events of Solomon's reign—all he did and the wisdom he displayed—are they not written in the book of the annals of Solomon? Solomon reigned in Jerusalem over all Israel forty years. Then he rested with his ancestors and was buried in the city of David his father. And Rehoboam his son succeeded him as king."

So, I like to think that as Solomon reflected on how things used to be between himself and God he realized that this life wasn't meaningless, and thus the reason (after "all had been heard," after he reflected on his life) why he came to his conclusion. And in doing so, he prompted his readers to take a hard look at those things they thought brought meaning to their lives.

Now all has been heard; here is the conclusion of the matter: Fear God and keep his commandments, for this is the duty of all mankind.

(ECCLESIASTES 12:13, NIV)

How to Find Meaning in a Meaningless Life

Lesson Six

Let go of past regrets, the *if onlys* of your life, and go forward with God.

Never forget that God loves you more than any human can. He is your true significant other who loves you and believes in you more than you can even begin to fathom.

> **"God demonstrates his own love for us in this: While we were still sinners, Christ died for us."**
>
> (ROMANS 5:8, NIV)

Let's Pray – Dear Lord, I know I cannot begin to comprehend the love you have for me. I truly want to love you as much as you love me, so please help me show my love through my obedience to your word. And, Father God, help me avoid the *if onlys* in my life. Turn my *if onlys* into You only! In Jesus' name, amen.

THE CONCLUSION

"As water reflects the face, so a man's heart reflects the man."
(PSALM 27:19, NIV)

When my nephew Bryce, who illustrated this study, first showed me his idea for the cover, I was blown away. I thought it was awesome. What he had to point out, however, was that the stars made a subtle cross. For some reason I missed that at first. As I pondered it further I thought to myself, *Couldn't we say the same about life's meaning?* It is right in front of us but we can easily miss it.

Of course, this drew me back to Solomon. The book of Ecclesiastes is either a cautionary tale of shallow pride and the consequence of life without God, or it is one from which we can gain rich insight into those things in life that are really important and give life meaning.

When Solomon was young (most scholars place his age at around twenty when he became king), he asked God for wisdom because he knew that at such a young age he would need all the help he could get. God gave him wisdom. In fact, God gave him "wisdom and very great insight, and a breadth of understanding as measureless as the sand on the seashore." (I King 4:29) Yet, for the most part, as we read through Ecclesiastes, it seemed easy to assume that Solomon left God behind (so to speak) at some point and, over time, became prideful regarding his own wisdom, wealth, and accomplishments. In doing so he became bitter about life. However,

Solomon knew God intimately. So, he either completely turned from God or, maybe, just maybe, as I suggested earlier, he turned back to God and wrote this book in an effort to stir the hearts of his readers to seek a more meaningful life. Remember, it is never too late to turn back to God!

Several years ago, the church I attend in Durango did a sermon series on *the seven deadly sins*. In case you aren't familiar with them, they are:

pride, envy, gluttony, lust, anger, greed, and sloth.

It was a great series, but the sermon I most remember was the one given by our young adult leader, Zack Esgar, on "sloth."(9) If you are like me, you most likely think of laziness when you hear the word "sloth." However, as I learned from Zack's message, "sloth" has a much deeper meaning, more along the lines of apathy and/or ungratefulness.

Zack painted a great mental picture of this when he described his first attempt to climb one of Colorado's many 14,000-foot mountains, Mt. Blanca. This impressive mountain in Alamosa, CO, upon reaching its top, allows spectacular views of over seven million acres below. (Did you catch that? Seven million acres!) From Zack's telling, it is breathtaking! However, when he reached the top and was taking in these views, there was a group ahead of him who were looking at a dark line of smoke off in the distance. They were commiserating among themselves as to what might be the cause and were distressed to think that it might be the result of someone, far, far away, burning rubber tires or something.

The point? With all of the stunning views on which these people could focus, they chose to fix their attention on the small line of darkness in the sky. Can you relate? All too often we focus on the one negative, the small line of darkness in our lives. In doing so we tend to miss the breathtaking beauty of creation that surrounds us, the goodness that dwells in the hearts of most of people, the tiny miracles that God brings us each and every day, and the incomprehensible promises that God has made us. We miss the simple and yet profound meaning that God gives to the life of the believer. God has given us the blessing of life here on earth and the hope of life eternal, yet we often forget our blessings, focus on the dark line in our lives, and, in essence, say to our creator that life is meaningless. Can you imagine how much this grieves God?

I feel certain that you would not want to purposely grieve God any more than I do; thus, the reason for this study. The scripture from Psalms that I quoted at the beginning of the conclusion, "As water reflects the face, so a man's heart reflects the man," should get us thinking. Are our hearts reflecting the one dark line in our lives or are we reflecting God's glory?

The subtitle *Finding Meaning in a Meaningless Life* is another way of saying always remember what is really important in life and glorify God in all circumstances.

Thus, I hope this study causes you to ask yourself the question, are you grieving God by thinking that life is meaningless, or are you glorifying God by your gratefulness?

Finally, I have to admit that I still see the book of Ecclesiastes as a rather odd duck, but I am glad we went duck hunting! I hope you are, too.

E(EEK)CCLESIASTES

How to Find Meaning in a Meaningless Life

1. Always seek godly wisdom.
2. Remember that life here on earth is short; eternity is forever.
3. Don't focus on what you have; focus on whose you are.
4. Quite chasing after the wind and chase after the Spirit.
5. Be still and know that God is God (and you're not).
6. Continually thank God for your many blessings.
7. Be at peace with who you are, seeking only God's approval and not man's.
8. Never forget God's mercy.
9. Maintain your balance by developing a strong core character.
10. Remember that you are a saint.
11. Know that your hope will not disappoint you, because God does not lie.
12. Keep in mind that once you leave this life, you will be with God forever.
13. Let go of past regrets and move forward with God.
14. Never doubt how much God loves you!

"May the God of hope fill you with all joy and peace as you trust in Him, so that you may overflow with hope by the power of the Holy Spirit."

(ROMANS 15:13, NIV)

Love, Joyce

A Special Thanks to

One thing I inadvertently failed to do when I published my last study was to say "thank you" to some people. So, I wanted to be sure to thank some folks who helped with my last study and those who came through for me again.

I thank each and every one of you for taking the time to help complete this study!

My niece, Rebecca (Becky) Walawander, for all her help with the design/layout of my other studies, for designing my website, for getting my studies on eBay, and Essie and for her ongoing encouragement

Bryce Cree, my nephew, for the great job he did illustrating this study

Will Ridout, who did the artwork for my *What Do You Really Want?* study on prayer

Amy Fidel and Bonnie Catalano for faithfully completing the study while still in its original draft form in order to catch my mistakes, make suggestions, and also offer encouragement

The Gift Group for going through numerous studies with me while in rough form, making sure my questions and comments made sense and for always being there for me

Katy Pickard and Diana Andrews for their prayers

Pastor Dale Roddey for allowing me to lead my studies at Crossroads Church

Last, but definitely not least, the Lord God Almighty! I thank Him for His continual guidance and love, and for giving me the gift of writing, thus making this and all of my studies possible. To Him be all glory and honor! Amen.

CREDITS

(1) Billy Crystal's Monologue, The Midlife Crisis, from *City Slickers*, a Castle Rock production, released in 1991 by Columbia Pictures.

(2) Lemmel, Helen R. "Turn Your Eyes Upon Jesus," copyright 1922 and renewal c 1949 by Singsperation Music. Taken from **Worship His Majesty** (hymnal), copyright 1987 by Gaither Music Company, Inc. Alexandra, Indiana 46001.

(3) Seeger, Peter. "Turn! Turn! Turn! (to Everything There Is a Season)," recorded by The Byrds, December 6, 1965 under the Columbia/Legacy label, copyright 1996 Sony Music Entertainment, Inc.

(4) A quote by A. A. Milne, author of the Winnie-the-Pooh books.

(5) Shakespeare, William. *The Merchant of Venice*. These lines have been taken in part from Portia's speech, which occurs during Act IV, Scene 1.

(6) Blackaby, Henry T. and Claude V. King. *Experiencing God: Knowing and Doing the Will of God*. Lifeway Church Resources, copyright 1990, LifeWay Press.

(7) Warren, Tish Harrison. *Liturgy of the Ordinary: Sacred Practices in Everyday Life*. Andy Crouch (foreword), November 1, 2016, IV Press.

(8) Rodrick, Stephen. "Chris Rock talks divorce, admits to infidelity

and says he wants to find God," Fox News Entertainment online article, published May 03, 2017, taken from *Rolling Stone* magazine.

(9) From Zack Esgar's August 18, 2013 sermon on Sloth, at First Methodist Church of Durango, CO. http://www.fumcdurango. org/sermons/sloth/

CPSIA information can be obtained
at www.ICGtesting.com
Printed in the USA
LVHW06s0414061018
592609LV00003B/8/P